It's Christmas!

It's Christmas!

A SELECTION OF FOUR STORIES
WRITTEN BY ALEXA TEWKESBURY

CWR

The Christmas Star's Big Shine
Text copyright © Alexa Tewkesbury 2005
Illustrations copyright © CWR 2005
Illustrations by Steve Boulter
Published 2005 by CWR

What's Christmas?
Text copyright © Alexa Tewkesbury 2006
Illustrations copyright © CWR 2006
Illustrations by Steve Boulter
Published 2006 by CWR

The Perfect Christmas Present
Text copyright © Alexa Tewkesbury 2008
Illustrations copyright © Hannah Wood 2008
Illustrations by Hannah Wood
Published 2008 by CWR

The Camel Who Found Christmas
Text copyright © Alexa Tewkesbury 2007
Illustrations copyright © CWR 2007
Illustrations by Steve Boulter
Published 2007 by CWR

This reformatted edition published 2013 by CWR, Waverley Abbey House, Waverley Lane, Farnham, Surrey GU9 8EP, UK.
Registered Charity No. 294387. Registered Limited Company No. 1990308.
The right of Alexa Tewkesbury to be identified as the author of this work has been asserted by her in accordance with the Copyright, Designs and Patents Act 1988.
All rights reserved. No part of this publication may be reproduced, stored in a retrieval system, or transmitted, in any form or by any means, electronic, mechanical, photocopying, recording or otherwise, without the prior permission in writing of CWR.
Concept development, editing, design and production by CWR
For a list of National Distributors visit www.cwr.org.uk/distributors
Printed in China by 1010 Printing International
ISBN: 978-1-85345-994-8

Contents

The Christmas Star's Big Shine	7
What's Christmas?	37
The Perfect Christmas Present	67
The Camel Who Found Christmas	97

The Christmas Star's Big Shine

The night was still. Little Star flickered sleepily in the velvet sky.

Suddenly –

'Wake up!'

He opened his eyes with a start. An angel was nudging him with a shimmer-white wing.

'Come on, rise and shine,' the angel chivvied.

'You've got an important job to do.'

'Have I?' whispered Little Star.

'A very special baby boy is about to be born in Bethlehem,' announced the angel.

'He's the Son of God, and He'll bring happiness to people all over the world.'

'Really?' murmured Little Star.

'Really,' said the angel. 'His name will be Jesus, and God wants *you* to let everyone know He's here.'

'Me?' gasped Little Star.

'Yes, you,' said the angel. 'You'd better get a move on.'

Little Star looked worried.

'But where do I go?' he asked.

'Bethlehem,' the angel replied as he flew off into the night. 'He'll be born in a stable there.'

'And how do I tell people?' called Little Star.

'Simple,' the angel called back. 'You just shine.'

Little Star thought for a moment.
'If God wants me to shine, I'll be the shiniest star in the whole universe,' he twinkled.
'Shining's what I do.'
Then he took a deep breath and –

'WHEEEEE!'

He shot off through the velvet sky, whizzing over fields and forests, across rivers and streams. 'Little Star coming through. Got an important job to do!'

Little Star zipped over swirling seas and flat, dusty
plains. He was just zooming across a hot, steamy
jungle when a cheeky voice said,
'You're in a hurry.'
Little Star called down,
'Can't stop. Got to fly. On a mission to light up the sky!'
'What for?' asked the voice.
'To tell everyone about God's new baby,' replied
Little Star proudly. 'Are we in Bethlehem?'
'Not really,' said the voice. 'This is Africa. But I'll
help you find the way.'

Little Star peered through the tangle of trees and creepers straight into the eyes of –

A MONKEY.

'I won't be any trouble,' Monkey said. He scrambled to the top of a very tall tree, grasped Little Star's gleaming tail and –

WHEEESH!

They scooted off through the velvet sky. They flashed across a huge ocean and skimmed over a rich, leafy rainforest.

'Looks like fun,' rumbled a voice.
Little Star called down,
'Can't stop. Got to fly. On a mission to light up the sky!'
'Can I help?' purred the voice.
Monkey chirped, 'Is this Bethlehem?'
'Oh no,' replied the voice. 'This is India. Will that do?'
'Not tonight,' said Little Star. 'I've got to tell everyone about God's new baby.'
'Mind if I join you?' asked the voice.
Little Star and monkey peeped through the juicy green leaves and found themselves face to face with –

A TIGER.
'I'll be quiet as a mouse,' he promised.
So Tiger took hold of Monkey, Monkey grasped
Little Star's tail and —

SWISSSH!!

They dashed away through the velvet sky.
They soared over mighty mountains, then scurried across shadowy forests of thick bamboo.

'Got room for one more?' asked a hopeful voice.
Little Star called down,
'Can't stop. Got to fly. On a mission to light up the sky!'
'Is it dangerous?' enquired the voice.
'Not dangerous,' said Little Star, 'but very important.
Is this Bethlehem?'
'Good gracious, no,' answered the voice, 'this is China.
Bethlehem's that way. Shall I show you?'
Little Star, Monkey and Tiger all squinted down
and there, peeking back up at them was –

A PANDA.

'Yes, please,' cried Little Star. 'I've got to tell everyone about God's new baby.'

So Panda took hold of Tiger, Tiger held onto Monkey, Monkey grasped Little Star's tail and —

PHIZZZZ!!

They rushed off through the velvet sky.
Faster and faster they flew.
Then suddenly —

'Look out!'
An angel shot out of the sky in front of them.
'We're going to crash!' squealed Monkey.
Little Star shuddered and juddered and screeched and –

Stopped. Just in time.

'Terribly sorry,' said the angel, 'but I've got to spread some amazing news so I can't hang about.'

Little Star's eyes opened wide.

'Has Jesus been born?' he asked.

The angel looked puzzled. 'Only just. How did you know?'

'*I've* got to spread the news too,' Little Star grinned.

The angel pointed down to a small, scruffy stable.

'Jesus is asleep in there with His mother, Mary, and Joseph, her husband,' he smiled. 'One day He'll rescue people from all the bad things in their lives and bring them close to God.'

Little Star beamed. 'So this must be where I'm supposed to shine.'

'Definitely,' said the angel. 'Anyway, must dash. I've got to give some shepherds the good news.' Then winking at Little Star, the angel added 'Enjoy your Big Shine', and flew away.

'My Big Shine,' thought Little Star. Then –

'Oh no!' he cried. 'Supposing I'm too small. God wants me to shine brightly enough to let everyone know about His wonderful new baby. But what if I can't? What if nobody notices?'

'Of course everyone will notice,' replied Monkey. '*We* all noticed you, didn't we?'

So Little Star closed his eyes, puffed out his chest and began to shine as he'd never shone before. At first he only glimmered.

But then the glimmer grew into a glow ...

and the glow began to beam ...

and soon the beam became a gleam ...

and all of a sudden Little Star burst into the most dazzling shine of his life!

'Am I doing it?' he shouted.
'Yes!' shrieked the animals. 'Look!'
Far, far away, three wise-looking
men were pointing at Little Star.
Then they each picked up a present
for the baby Jesus and set off to
find Him, following Little Star's
glaring trail.

'They all want to see Jesus,' cried Monkey,
'and they'll find Him because of you, Little Star.'
Some shepherds were gazing at Little Star too.
His radiant light guided them right to the stable door.

Little Star glittered with glee, and the velvet sky blazed in the brilliant light of the biggest shine the world would ever see.

What's Christmas?

It was daylight. Snow Bear stretched and yawned and poked her small black nose out of her den. Old Polar was already up.

'What are you doing, Old Polar?' asked Snow Bear.
'I was just thinking,' Old Polar replied.
'Thinking what?' queried Snow Bear.
'I was just thinking,' answered Old Polar, 'that it must be nearly Christmas.'
'Christmas?' Snow Bear looked puzzled. 'What's Christmas?'
Old Polar's dark eyes twinkled in his white fur like two glass beads.
'Don't you know?' he mused. 'Then it's time you found out, Snow Bear.' And he ambled away.

Snow Bear sat down and her small black nose twitched in the freezing air.

There was a sudden explosion of snow in front of her.
An arctic hare shot past in a flurry of white.

'Excuse me,' Snow Bear called, and the flurry skidded to a halt.
'Are you talking to me?' the hare asked crisply.

'Yes,' answered Snow Bear, lolloping over.
'Can you tell me, please – what's Christmas?'
The hare's whiskers quivered in the pale morning light.
'Don't you know?' he replied. 'Christmas is a girl called Mary riding on a donkey to a town far away, with a very special present.'

Snow Bear frowned.
'What's that supposed to mean?'
'It means what it says,' declared the hare and, with a flip and a scurry, he was gone.

Snow Bear padded thoughtfully across the winter plains until she came to the cold, calm ocean. The brownish blob of a walrus bobbed up to the surface.

'Hello, Snow Bear,' greeted the blob. 'Want to play?'
'I can't today,' Snow Bear replied. 'I'm trying to find out something very important. Can *you* tell me – what's Christmas?'
The walrus's tusks gleamed against the ice-blue sea. 'Don't you know?' she remarked. 'Christmas is nowhere to stay, just a damp, dingy stable where a tiny new baby lies sleeping in the straw.'
Snow Bear's face fell.
'But that doesn't make sense,' she complained.

'It will,' assured the walrus
and, with a flop and a splash, she swam away.

Snow Bear trudged slowly along by the water's edge. Something brightly coloured caught her eye. A puffin was watching her curiously.
'Can I help you?' the puffin enquired.
'I shouldn't think so,' mumbled Snow Bear.
'Please let me try,' he persisted.

Snow Bear sighed. 'It's just that I'm trying to understand – what's Christmas?'
The puffin's beak shone like a jewel under the paper-white sky. 'Don't you know?' he chuckled. 'Christmas is a sky full of angels cheering and singing, and shepherds on a hillside setting off to meet a King.'
Snow Bear shook her head impatiently.
'But that doesn't mean anything,' she moaned.
'There *must* be something more.'

'Oh, there is,' smiled the puffin. 'Something much more.' And, with a flap and a flutter, he flew away.

Snow Bear's small black nose
felt cold and damp.
'It's no good,' she muttered,
'I'll never understand Christmas,'
and she plonked herself down on
the frozen ground.

'Christmas?' chirped a cheery voice.
'What do you want to know?'

A boy stood in front of her, his shiny, round face peering out through a muffle of fur.
Snow Bear blinked in the frost-sharp air.

'Well,' she began, 'I know there was Mary and a donkey and a very special present.

I know there was nowhere to stay and a baby in a stable.

I even know there were angels, and some shepherds who went to meet a King.
But what I *don't* know is —

What's Christmas?'

The boy smiled. 'But, Snow Bear, that *is* Christmas,' and he sat down beside her and told her how Mary had ridden the donkey to a faraway town called Bethlehem, and how the present was her baby, born in a stable one starry night because there was nowhere for them to stay. He told her how angels had filled the skies over the hilltops, calling the shepherds to go and visit the King, and how the King was the newborn baby, lying sleeping in the straw.

Snow Bear's eyes glistened and her small black nose trembled with excitement.
'Then I've got it!' she cried. 'Christmas is the King's birthday!'

'Don't you want to know His name?' asked the boy as Snow Bear turned to gallop home.
'What is it?' she called.
'Jesus!' the boy announced. 'The baby King's called Jesus!'

Snow Bear raced away and when she found Old Polar, she tumbled against his soft white tummy and laughed, 'I know! I know!'

'What do you know, Snow Bear?' asked Old Polar, wrapping her up in his great shaggy paws.

'I know what Christmas is,' Snow Bear beamed. 'It's the King's birthday.'

'Well done,' said Old Polar. 'And do you know what Christmas is most of all?'

'You mean there's more?' Snow Bear gasped.

'Much more,' replied Old Polar. 'Most of all, Christmas is love. God's love. The baby King is His Son, and God loves everyone so much that He gave them His very own baby to bring peace and happiness to the whole world.'

'Wow!' murmured Snow Bear, wrinkling her small black nose in amazement. 'God must love everybody a huge amount.'
'Oh, yes,' Old Polar nodded. 'Indeed He does.'

The Perfect Christmas Present

I first saw a troop of sleepy Aldabra Giant Tortoises at Paignton Zoo and they were so magnificent that I instantly wanted to write one into a story. Because they come from the Seychelles, it seemed appropriate to set this tale in their homeland, so I needed to find another creature who lives there to be a companion. Being small and excitable, the Common Tenrec Shrew seemed to fit the bill perfectly – providing an ideal contrast with the huge, cumbersome tortoise.

Alexa Tewkesbury

A community of around 152,000 **Aldabra Giant Tortoises** currently live on the Aldabra Atoll in the Seychelles. Among the biggest tortoises in the world, they grow to some 120cm in length and often live for well over one hundred years. Although it's in their nature to be rather careful and slow, they can put on a burst of speed if they happen to spot something tasty to eat, and are also very skilled swimmers.

The **Common Tenrec Shrew** is found in Madagascar and western central Africa, and from there has been introduced to the islands of the Seychelles in the Indian Ocean. It can grow to between 29cm and 36cm long, is greyish to reddy-brown in colour, with a paler tummy, and has little ears and a long, pointed snout. Tenrec Shrews tend to prefer living by themselves, and enjoy feasts of worms and insects.

Under a smooth, flat stone in the snuggest, driest hole on the hilltop hid Small, fast asleep. Night had fallen, cool and calm and quiet. Then …

'What?' squealed Small, snapping suddenly wide awake. The bristly, bumbling shrew blinked uncomfortably and screwed up his eyes. A curious light was flooding his snug, dry hole.

Small was not happy.
'I'm *not* happy,' he muttered. 'It's supposed to be night. Cool and calm and quiet. What's all this light?'

His long snout snuffled huffily and he peeped crossly out from under the smooth, flat stone. The most dazzling sight met his tiny, bright eyes.

Far up in the sky glittered a huge star and everywhere glistened silver in its marvellous light.
Small scrambled to the top of a large, knobbly rock to get a better view all around.

'Beautiful, isn't it?' murmured the rock.
But then a wise,
crinkly head turned and peered up at him with two smiling, dark eyes, and Small realised it wasn't a rock at all. It was a giant of a tortoise.
'So sorry!' Small mumbled.
'Happens all the time,' replied the giant kindly. 'Think nothing of it.'
Over their heads, the huge star flashed and gleamed.

'I've never seen anything like it,' remarked Small.

'It's a message,' declared the giant. 'From God.'

'What message?' asked Small.

The giant's smiling, dark eyes shone in the starlight. 'He's arrived,' she announced. 'It's Christmas, and here on earth a baby called Jesus has been born. God's very own Son.'

Small frowned. 'But why would God's Son be born on earth?'

'To grow up with us and share His life with us,' answered the giant, 'and, most of all, to bring us close to God. Jesus is God's gift to the world.' Small shuffled excitedly on his sharp-clawed feet.

'Then I must get going,' he exclaimed. 'If God loves us enough to give us His very own baby Son, I must find Him an amazing present to say thank you.'

'But …' began the giant.
'This is no time for stargazing,' interrupted Small, sliding down from the tortoise's large, knobbly shell.

'It's just ...' continued the giant.
'Must dash,' huffed Small, landing neatly on the ground on his four short legs.

'If you'd only let me explain ...' insisted the giant, gently. 'Places to go, presents to find!' sang Small, and he scuttled away into the silvery night, rooting through grass and snuffling among leaves.

At last he spied a berry, red and glossy and round as the full moon.
'That's it!' cried Small. 'That's the perfect present … or is it?'
High above him, the huge star beamed down on the round, red berry.
Then, 'No!' he squeaked. 'How can a round, red berry be enough?
God's gift to the world is *so* much bigger!'

Small scampered on, skipping between tree roots and bustling under bushes, until his eye was caught by a feather, soft and sleek and light as a wisp of cloud.
'That's it!' shrieked Small.
'That's the perfect present … or is it?'

The soft, sleek feather shimmered in the glow from the huge star. Then, 'No, no!' he piped. 'How can a soft, sleek feather be enough? God's gift to the world is so much bigger!'

Small skittered off down the hillside, and beyond the bumpy tussocks of grass at its foot stretched a beautiful, sandy beach. There, at the edge of the sea, lay a shell, curled and pale and creamy as a new pearl.
'Now that's *got* to be it!' he screeched. 'That's *got* to be the perfect present!'
So, pushing with his long snout, then pulling with his sharp-clawed feet, he rolled and dragged the shell over a dune and along the beach, until he was quite out of breath.

He found the giant lying under a tree.
'Look!' puffed Small. 'Look what I've found!
The perfect present for God!'
In the skies overhead, the huge star sparkled and washed the pale, creamy shell in its burning light – and, all of a sudden, the shell seemed too little.

'No, no, NO!' grumbled Small, dismally. 'This is all wrong. How can a pale, creamy shell be enough? God's gift to the world is *so* much bigger!'
The giant's smiling, dark eyes twinkled in the starshine.
'Cheer up,' she soothed. 'I tried to tell you before – but you were in such a hurry.'
Then she lifted her wise, crinkly head and explained to the bristly, bustling shrew that he didn't have to chase around a hilltop searching out the perfect present for God.
The perfect present was here all the time.

'It's you,' the giant said. 'It's me. It's everyone living on the earth. This Christmas night, God's given Himself to the world by sending His baby Son to live here. The only present He wants in return ... is us.' Small was puzzled.

Up and away, the huge star glinted and winked, and another light was beginning to creep silently across the sky. A new morning was on its way.

Under a smooth, flat stone in the snuggest,
driest hole on the hilltop sat Small, wide awake.
'Thank You for giving us Jesus, Lord God,'
he whispered happily.
'Now, here am I. All for You.'

The Camel who found Christmas

It was time. Deep in the night
under a star-bright sky,
three wise men had loaded up their three tall
camels and were ready to begin their journey.
But the littlest camel was still fast asleep.
Mama Camel nuzzled him with her silky nose.
'Time to go, little one,' she whispered.

The littlest camel blinked dreamily.
'Time to go where?'
'It's Christmas,' Mama Camel replied. 'Look up in the sky. We're following a star to meet a king.'
'What king?' the littlest camel asked.
'The most important king in the world,' murmured Mama Camel. 'Jesus, the Son of God.'

The littlest camel frowned and shook his head. 'Then I can't come with you,' he sighed. 'Why would a king want to meet me? I'm just not big enough.'

Mama Camel's eyes were soft and kind.
'Nonsense!' she said. 'Everyone's big enough to meet King Jesus.'
So the three wise men set off riding their three tall camels, and the littlest camel trotted quietly along behind.

But as shadows flickered silently in the starlight all around, the littlest camel began to think – 'Supposing the king lives in a huge, glittering palace, with stately walls and marvellous towers, and hundreds of candles to light the hundreds of stairs.

How can I possibly go there? A royal palace is no place for a camel like me.'

And the still night air felt colder and colder, and the littlest camel felt smaller and smaller, and at last he called out, 'It's no good, I can't come with you. Why would a king want to meet me? I'm just not important enough.'

Mama Camel's voice was gentle and calm. 'Silly!' she soothed. 'Everyone's important enough to meet King Jesus.'
So the three tall camels carrying the three wise men travelled on, and the littlest camel trekked slowly along behind.

But as the clouds threaded their wispy way between the twinkling stars, and the only sound was the *flomp flomp* of the camels' feet on the sandy ground, he began to wonder –

'Supposing the king's friends are all rich and grand, with rippling robes and rustling cloaks, and rows of jewels gleaming on their delicate fingers and toes. How can I possibly visit the king with them? They'd want nothing to do with a camel like me.'

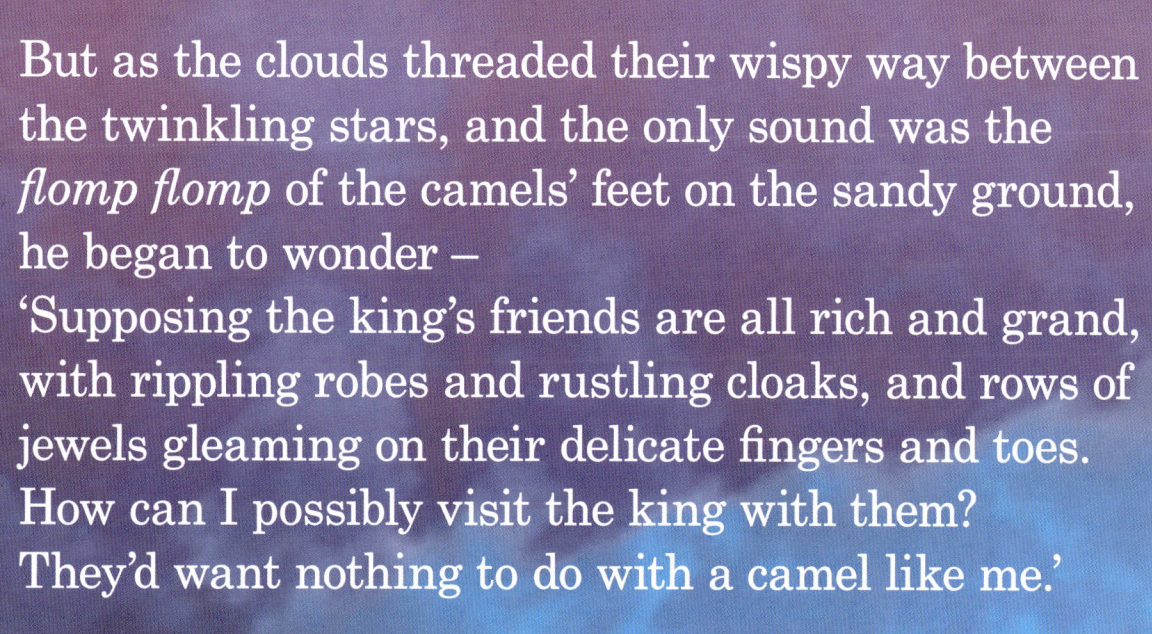

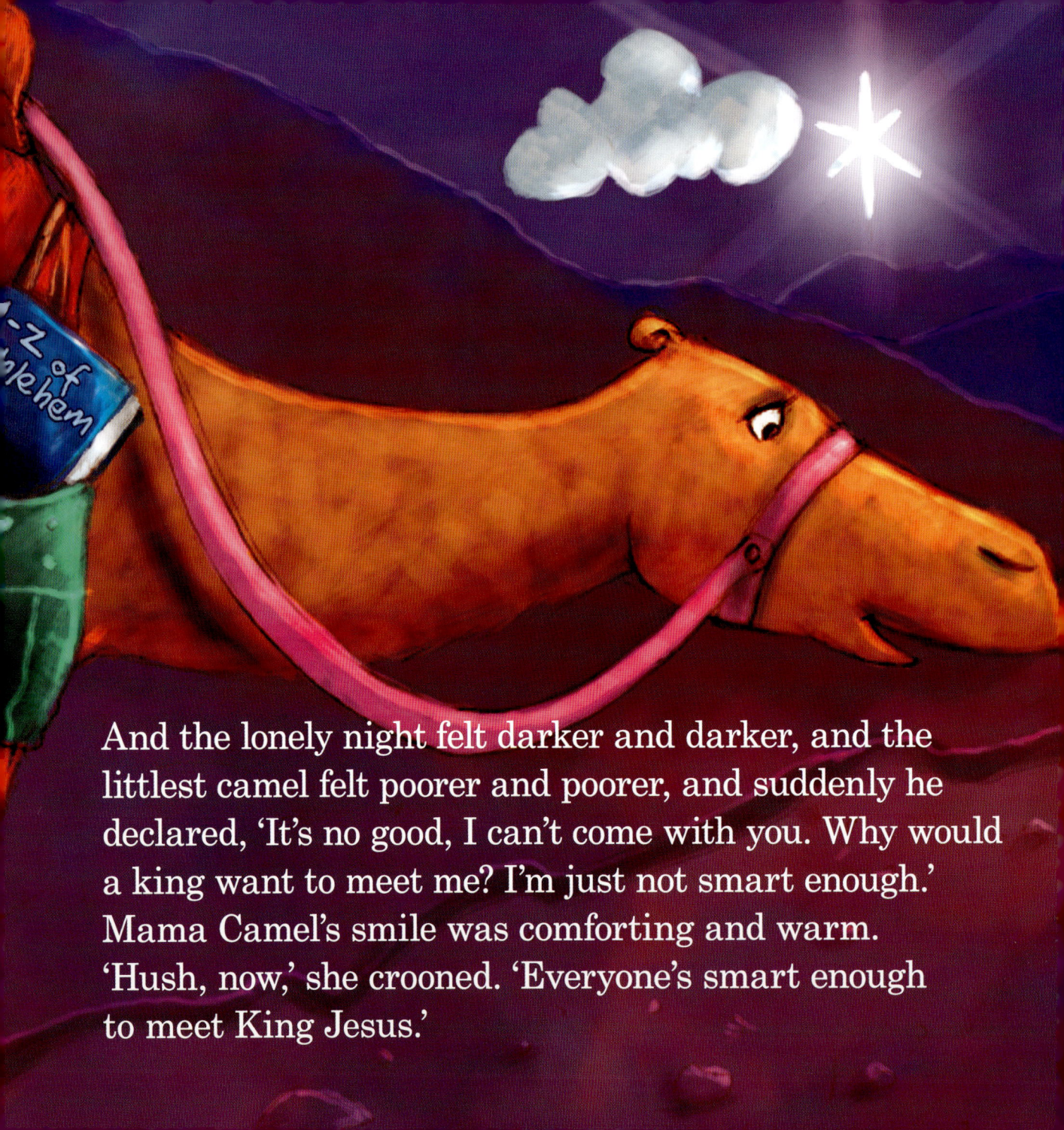

And the lonely night felt darker and darker, and the littlest camel felt poorer and poorer, and suddenly he declared, 'It's no good, I can't come with you. Why would a king want to meet me? I'm just not smart enough.' Mama Camel's smile was comforting and warm. 'Hush, now,' she crooned. 'Everyone's smart enough to meet King Jesus.'

He began to grow tired and a chilly breeze ruffled his short, brown coat.
'Mama Camel,' he asked, 'how much further is the king?'
'As far as the star takes us,' Mama Camel replied.
Then the littlest camel began to worry –
'Supposing the king is fierce and proud, with cold, hard eyes and a brilliant kingly crown on his dazzling kingly head! How can I possibly stand in front of him? A mighty king will have no time for a camel like me.'

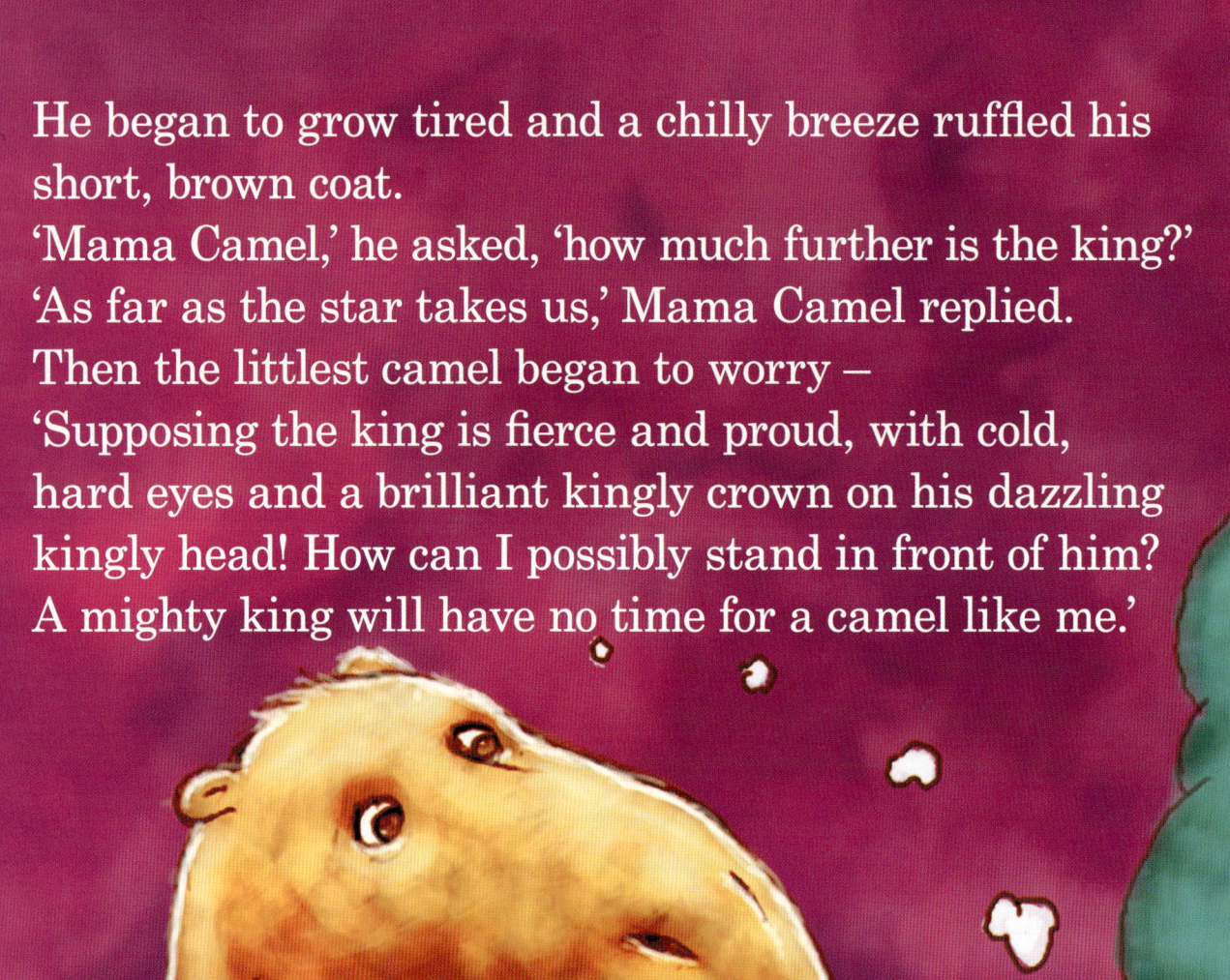

And the littlest camel felt sadder and sadder, and his small, dusty feet plodded slower and slower, until finally Mama Camel asked, 'What's the matter, little one?'
'It's no good,' he sniffed, 'I can't come with you. Why would a king want to meet me? I'm just not special enough.'

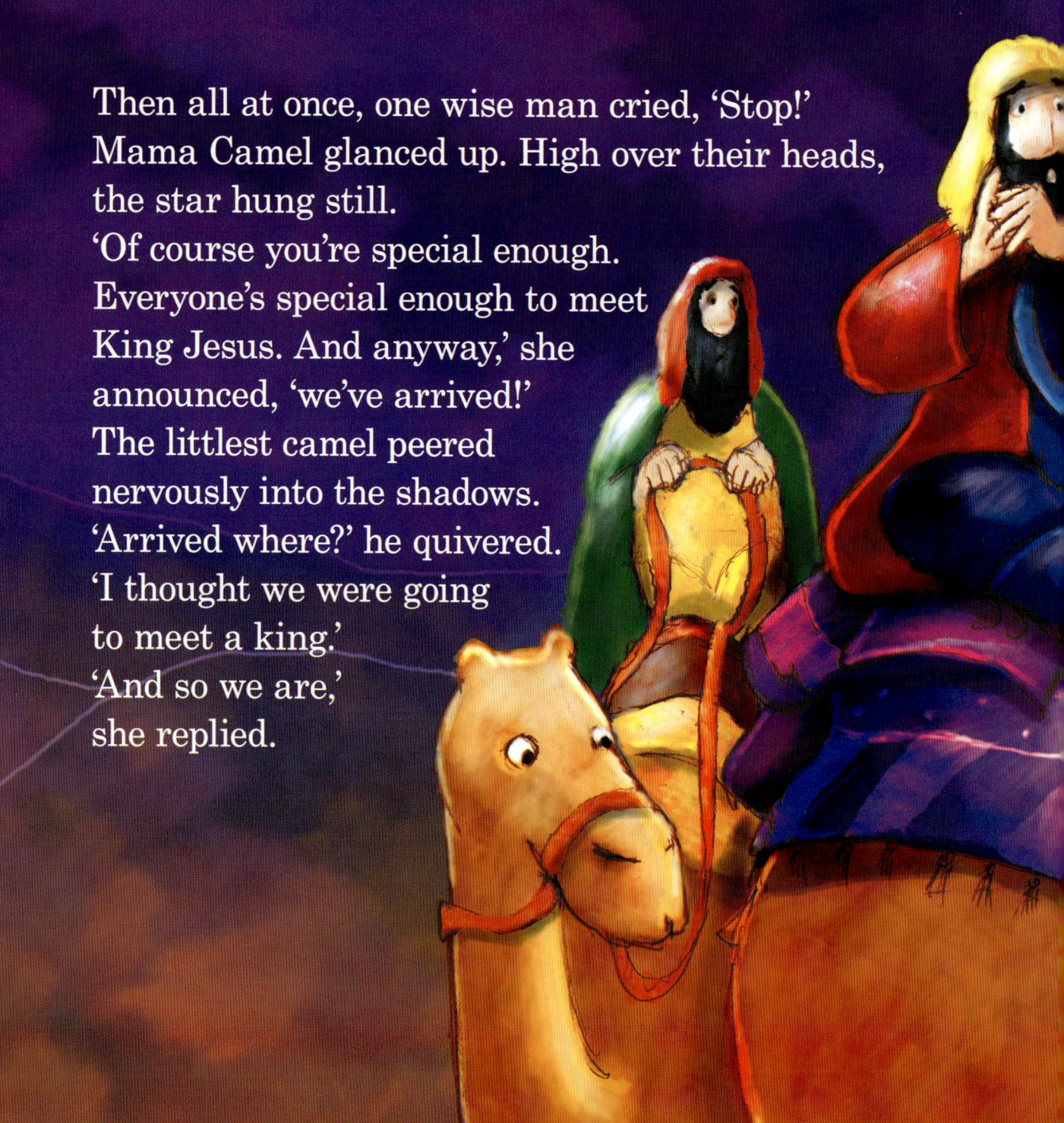

Then all at once, one wise man cried, 'Stop!' Mama Camel glanced up. High over their heads, the star hung still.
'Of course you're special enough. Everyone's special enough to meet King Jesus. And anyway,' she announced, 'we've arrived!'
The littlest camel peered nervously into the shadows.
'Arrived where?' he quivered.
'I thought we were going to meet a king.'
'And so we are,' she replied.

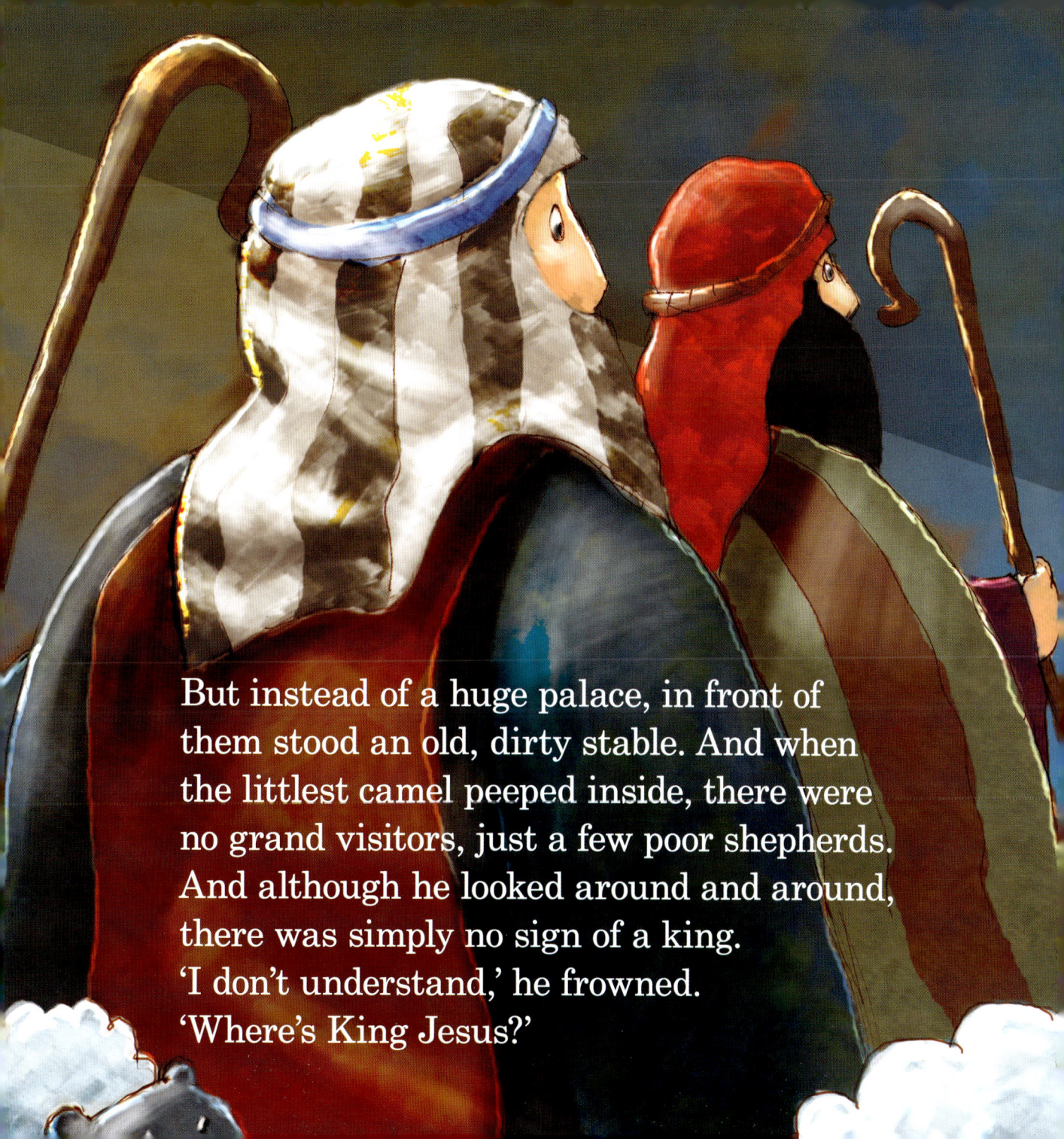

But instead of a huge palace, in front of them stood an old, dirty stable. And when the littlest camel peeped inside, there were no grand visitors, just a few poor shepherds. And although he looked around and around, there was simply no sign of a king.
'I don't understand,' he frowned.
'Where's King Jesus?'

Mama Camel's face was radiant with delight.
'There,' she murmured. 'Right there.'
And there, right there, fast asleep on a jumble of damp, dusty straw lay the tiniest new baby.

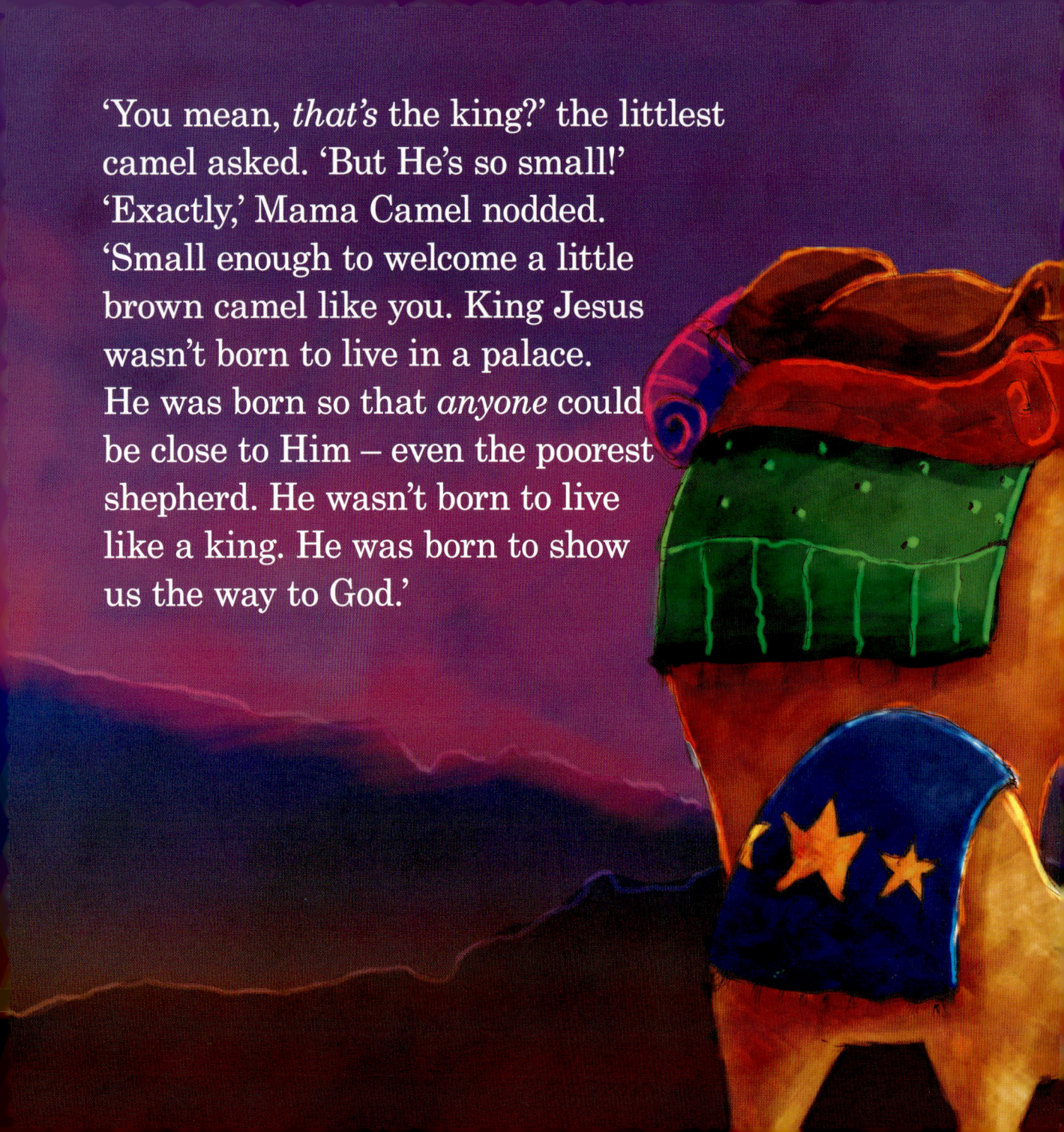

'You mean, *that's* the king?' the littlest camel asked. 'But He's so small!' 'Exactly,' Mama Camel nodded. 'Small enough to welcome a little brown camel like you. King Jesus wasn't born to live in a palace. He was born so that *anyone* could be close to Him – even the poorest shepherd. He wasn't born to live like a king. He was born to show us the way to God.'

For one hushed moment, the littlest camel stood thinking. Then his ears began to twitch and to tingle and a smile chased the frown from his little brown face. And as he crept closer to the tiny baby, he beamed, 'Then it's true! *Anyone* can meet King Jesus because King Jesus wants to meet EVERYONE!'

'Everyone everywhere,' Mama Camel replied. 'This is Christmas night – the night King Jesus was born for the whole world.'

More Books by Alexa Tewkesbury

Creative and fun for parents to use, reading *Pens* will help your preschool children enjoy daily Bible reading as they develop a love of God's Word. There are over 20 titles in the series, each ideal for 3 to 6 year olds. Pens bring the Bible to life with stories from Scripture and from their own experiences, combined with insightful comments, thought-provoking questions and simple prayers.

Join the Pens characters as they learn about the true meaning of Christmas in this special edition which is also available from **www.cwr.org.uk/pens** as an animated cartoon download. (Special editions for Easter, Starting School and Halloween also available.)

For more information and current prices please visit cwr.org.uk